Diana, another Royal scandal

David J Cooper

Published by David J Cooper, 2021.

DIANA, ANOTHER ROYAL SCANDAL

First edition. March 9, 2021.

Written by David J Cooper.

Also by David J Cooper

Penny Lane, Paranormal Investigator
The Witch Board
The House of Dolls
The House of Dolls
The Devil's Coins
The Mirror
The Key
The Reveal

Standalone
The Devil Knows
The Party's Over
Encuentro Mortal
Se Acabo La Fiesta
Cold Fury
Deadly Encounter
House on the Hill
Diana, another Royal scandal

Watch for more at davidjcooperauthorblog.wordpress.com.

Table of Contents

Foreword 1

Diana and Camilla 3

Diana - The Person. 9

History Repeating Itself. 15

Hypocrites.. 19

After the Divorce 23

Diana's Death 29

The Movie 31

Cause for Embarrassment? 33

Who Is to Blame? 35

Almost 25 years on 39

Will This Jigsaw Puzzle Ever Be Completed?........... 41

Reflections.. 43

Conclusion.. 45

Foreword

Diana Spencer was a lady by birth, a lady in waiting – waiting to become the next Queen of England. Tragically, that was not to be. The fairy tale wedding in 1981 brought hope to the British public that the monarchy would be radically changed forever when she became Queen. Tragically, the story didn't end like that. The fairy tale did not end happily ever after. It was a fairy tale that ended in disaster. The passing of time heals all wounds whether they are physical or emotional ones yet still leave scars. Some things are forgotten quite easily through time and some things are best forgotten even though memories linger on.

Diana and Camilla

Before Diana became involved with Prince Charles she was unknown. A shy young girl going about her daily life looking after small children.

Charles had been in a romantic relationship for years with Camilla before he met Diana and everybody thought that eventually he would marry Camilla. Charles and Camilla had so much in common. They both liked the country life, they both liked horses so they were an ideal match. Charles was very much in love with Camilla and obviously the love he had for her then continued right to the present day. He is now married to her.

Camilla is one year older than Charles so there isn't the age gap problem. There was a twelve year difference in age between him and Diana.

Diana had nothing in common with Charles.

There was the big difference in age – she was very young when she married him. He loved reading, the arts and preferred the country life, blood sports and the opera. She loved the city life, pop stars and glamour and she was your typical girl next door.

The marriage was doomed right from the start.

The only thing that Diana and Camilla had in common was Charles!!

Comparing Diana and Camilla is like making a comparison between Beauty and the Beast.

In the fairy-tale the Beast turned out to be a handsome prince but in this case the Beast turned out to be the other woman.

Diana's Prince Charming turned out to be Prince Charmless! How devastating for her to discover that he never loved her at all. She was a convenient baby making machine. Someone to produce a future heir to the throne. If Charles didn't love Diana why the hell did he marry her?

Diana cared while Camilla had no sense of shame. She knew what would happen when she started interfering in the marriage and becoming Charles' mistress. Could she care about Diana's feelings and the effect that it would have on her? Of course not!

Neither could Charles. He wasn't man enough to tell Diana that he didn't love her yet he had the nerve to go to Paris to identify her body! Not only did Camilla have a say in helping Charles choose Diana as his bride but she also helped him choose Highgrove the matrimonial home. How convenient as it was only a thirty minute drive from her own house – Raymill House. It made things very easy for them to continue with their clandestine affair.

Sadly, Diana was very much in love with Charles. She thought that he could give her the emotional stability she was looking for because he was more mature than her. On the other hand, for Charles it was a marriage of convenience.

Diana and Camilla were like chalk and cheese. Diana was the beauty. She had the looks of a model and was the most photographed woman. All the high fashion magazines carried her photos on their front covers. Camilla was the opposite. She had been referred to as the Rottweiler or the woman who looked like a horse.

In spite of all this, she was Charles' first and only real love. Well, Charles was no oil painting! Charles could not accept the fact that Camilla had rejected his marriage proposal years ago when they were both young. He could not accept that he had to find someone else to replace her because he had been in a relationship with her for such a long time and he still deeply loved her.

When Camilla re-appeared on the scene after he married Diana, he thought that he could take up where he left off and that because Camilla had been available to him all those years, she was available now regardless of Diana.

It has been claimed that Camilla encouraged Charles to marry Diana and helped him choose her as his bride. I cannot understand this because in Britain the British don't have arranged marriages. We are free to choose who we like. Having said that, in the Royal Family it is the norm for the Queen to need to accept and give her blessing to her children's choice of spouse so she usually has the last say in the matter.

As time went on, Camilla would live to regret this. Her former brother-in-law, Richard Parker-Bowles claimed that Camilla had encouraged the relationship between Charles and Diana because she thought that Diana was gormless. Because Diana was so young and naïve Camilla thought that she could be easily manipulated and never thought of Diana as being a threat. So later on all of this clever calculation was to backfire on her.

Diana wasn't as gormless as Camilla had thought and her intuition proved that Camilla had other motives but unfortunately, Diana wasn't to discover how important Camilla was for Charles until it was too late.

Diana was the beautiful one, very young and ripe to be able to produce an heir to the throne and Charles was there to fulfil his royal obligations – to sire an heir!! He also thought that Diana was the dumb blonde who could have his children and that he could manipulate her.

So, Charles and Camilla thought that they could manipulate Diana. They were very wrong and Diana retaliated when she refused to sit back and let things go on and let him get away with it.

She had grown and matured from the shy, little girl into a strong and determined and very outspoken woman. She had become very popular – more popular than the Queen, and it came as no surprise that many people felt that Charles had treated her very badly. He had betrayed her. If he didn't love her in the first place why the hell did he marry her?

Diana loved him very much but for him it was a marriage of convenience. I'm sure she didn't marry him just because he was the next in line to the throne – she was not the ambitious and calculating type of person but apparently the people who were the calculating ones were Charles and Camilla.

The more Diana became popular the more Charles hated it.

As Diana was no fool, she confronted Camilla telling her that she knew that Charles and she were having an affair. That takes some doing and I can only admire Diana for facing the problem head on.

She was not going to sit by and ignore it. Why should she? She was a human being trying to prevent another woman from stealing her husband, the man she truly loved. This is only natural. And how do you think Diana must have felt when she discovered that the woman who had encouraged Charles to marry her in the first place and believed that she was a friend was having an affair with him.

Having confronted Camilla only made things worse for Diana. It caused terrible rows between her and Charles. If Charles and Camilla had nothing to hide there wouldn't have been the ugly arguments. It proved to Diana that she meant nothing to Charles.

To top it all the Camilla gate tapes were made public in 1993 where Charles and Camilla spoke of their needing sex with each other several times a day.

The public turned against Charles and more so against Camilla who became imprisoned in her own home. When she went out she would be confronted by people and have things thrown at her and be cursed at by people. That was the feeling of the British public. Any hope of Charles had had of getting the nation to accept his relationship with Camilla had been dashed.

The Queen Mother also had her say in the matter. She was disgusted to discover that her favourite grandson had put his personal feelings or lusts before his duty to the crown. She refused to meet Camilla and didn't want to hear her name. As long as the Queen Mother was alive Charles had no hope in hell of marrying Camilla.

Another thing that the Queen Mother didn't like was the fact that Charles' relationship with Camilla had brought back bitter memories of the time her brother-in-law the Duke of Windsor was in his relationship with Wallis Simpson, which will be mentioned later on in the book.

Diana had a good relationship with the Queen Mother and the Queen Mother thought a lot of Diana.

After the Queen Mother's death in 2002 the Royals slowly began to accept Camilla and she began to make public appearances once more.

Diana - The Person.

Diana was a very well respected and much loved public person. She had everything: charm, charisma, grace and movie star looks. All the top women's' magazines carried her photos on their front covers. They followed her style and many women copied her mode of fashion and hairstyle. The media were forever hounding her.

Even though she was born with a title, a member of the aristocracy and affectionately known as Lady Di, she had no airs and graces about her. She was in fact quite ordinary. She was very attached to her father and his death devastated her.

She was a very compassionate woman and showed the world that she was an ordinary human being with feelings. Caring for people not as fortunate as her. She was charming and elegant, and had a very bubbly personality. She deeply loved Charles and was hurt very badly when their marriage started to disintegrate. She was the victim in a love triangle.

She mixed with people from all walks of life. She cared about people who had AIDS. She openly had physical contact with them, touching them, hugging them and not wearing gloves to demonstrate that this disease could not be transferred just by touching them. She danced with John Travolta when she visited the United States.

This surely tells us about the person she was another side to her personality. Her close friends were Elton John, Pavarotti and Versace.

She was a woman with many talents.

The following quotations made by Diana show us who she was and how she felt:

"Anywhere I see suffering, that is where I want to be, doing what I can."

"Being a princess isn't all it's cracked up to be."

"Carry out a random act of kindness, with no expectations of reward safe in the knowledge that one day someone might do the same for you."

"Every one of us needs to show how much we care for each other and, in the process, care for ourselves."

"Family is the most important thing in the world."

HIV does not make people dangerous to know, so you can shake their hands and give them a hug; Heaven knows they need it."

"Hugs can do great amounts of good – especially for children."

"I don't want expensive gifts; I don't want to be bought. I have everything I want. I just want someone to be there for me, to make me feel safe and secure."

"I like to be a free spirit. Some don't like that, but that's the way I am."

"I live for my sons. I would be lost without them."

"If you find someone you love in your life, then hang on to that love."

"Life is just a journey."

Those quotations show the real feelings of a person who is sincere. That's what Diana was, very sincere and very caring.

Many people placed her into the same category as Mother Teresa and Pope John Paul II.

Even though they were all very different people, they had one thing in common – caring for people, being close to people.

Diana cared for her family. She wanted her sons to have a normal upbringing, a normal childhood. She took them to theme parks, for example, so that they could enjoy the same things as any other child, even though they were of royal blood. This must have caused a headache for her security people, but it gave the boys a sense of freedom.

This is why she was so popular. She was a princess but she was also a mother.

How could anyone not like her?

Diana unravelled the "mystery" attached to the Royal Family. What is so mysterious about being royal? After all, they are a family – another family so why a mystery?

I remember when I saw the Queen for the first time in my life. I was a school boy and she came on a visit to the town where I was at high school. Her car passed near to the school and we all stood outside to see and salute her. She was very young then. I remember raising my cap to her as she went by in her large windowed Rolls Royce. I thought to myself. "This is the Queen of England, the mysterious person behind all of that glass." It was unbelievable to actually now see this person in real life. You only imagine that these people exist in fairy tales.

My history teacher presented her with a book he had written about the history of Wednesbury as a token of her visit.

Diana brought the Royal Family closer to the ordinary people by being physically among them. After all, she was an ordinary person even though she had the title of princess. The myth and the mystery of the Royal Family disappeared when Diana came on the scene. Now there was no "distance" between the public and the royals. They weren't people we just read about. They weren't people hidden away in palaces or in castles. They were real!

This is what she accomplished. The monarchy was now in touch with and connected with the people.

Diana said that she knew what her job as princess was. It was to go out and meet people and love them. She said that she would like to be a queen in people's hearts but that she didn't see herself as being the Queen of England because the establishment in to which she was married didn't like her. She said that it was vital that the monarchy kept in touch with the people and that was what she was trying to do.

She said that so many people had supported her through her public life and she would never forget them. She said that the kindness and affection from the public had carried her through some very difficult periods and that the love from the public had made it easier for her to continue.

She wanted so much that her marriage worked especially because she had come from divorced parents and wanted to work hard to make it work and not fall into the same pattern that she had seen happen in her own family. She said that she loved her husband very much and thought that they were a good team.

Sadly, a marriage is not a one sided affair. It can only succeed if the two people involved are putting in the same effort to make it survive.

This was not the case where Diana's marriage was concerned.

Diana said in her famous interview with the BBC when questioned about the break up, quote:

"Well, there were three of us in this marriage, so it was a bit crowded."

More sadly for her this had been going on for years, ever since she got married.

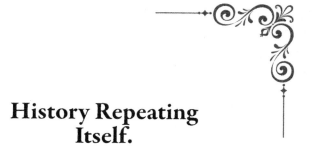

History Repeating Itself.

I f we look at the history of the British monarchy we can see that there was evil within it.

Henry VIII got rid of his wives once he had had enough of them by having them beheaded.

As he was King of England and had created the Church of England for his own convenience he had the power to do what he liked. Any excuse to get rid of one wife to enable him to marry another.

Then there was the case of Prince Albert Victor, grandson of Queen Victoria, who was suspected of being the infamous Jack the Ripper, although it was never proved. He happened to also be the eldest son of the then Prince of Wales!

But to bring us more up to date let's look at how history has repeated itself and the similarities that have given cause for embarrassment for the Royal Family.

It's strange how history seems to repeat itself and there have been two other similar and embarrassing events for the Royal Family during the last century.

The first happened back in the 1930s when Edward VIII abdicated the throne to marry Wallis Simpson.

The government at that time declared that a king could not marry a divorced person and so he was given a choice. He could be crowned as King of England and deny the woman he loved or he could the woman he loved and deny the throne.

He chose the latter, putting his feelings first and not his royal duties.

His brother Prince George, Queen Elizabeth's father became King George.

This would change history. Had Edward decided to deny Wallis and continue as King of England, Elizabeth probably would never have become Queen of England.

Edward marrying Wallis, a divorced American was a scandal in the eyes of the government and didn't go down very well with the Queen Mother.

So, Edward gave up the throne, married Wallis and lived in exile in Paris until his death in 1972. He was given the title of Duke of Windsor. Wallis was given the title of Duchess of Windsor but could not be referred to as Her Royal Highness.

The second incident involved Princess Margaret, the Queen's sister. Back in the 1950s Princess Margaret had a love affair with Group Captain Peter Townsend who was sixteen years older than her. He was a married man who eventually got divorced. She was desperately in love with him and wanted to marry him. The problem was that he was now divorced even though he was the innocent party it was not the done thing for a royal to marry a divorced person.

Princess Margaret was very much in love with Peter Townsend and wanted to marry him but the Queen wouldn't allow this because he was divorced. How strange that she gave her blessing to Charles, her son, heir to the throne, to marry

Camilla yet both of them were divorced. Camilla was the third party named by Diana as the cause of her marriage breakup.

It appears, in my opinion, and this is only my opinion, that the Queen can make changes as and when it suits her. Am I hearing echoes of Henry VIII?

After all is said and done all of her children are divorced, that is apart from Prince Edward.

As Diana once said and quote: "I will never become Queen because the establishment to which I am married doesn't want me to become Queen." We all know that the establishment that she referred to meant the Royal Family.

How sad! It was very convenient for her to produce an heir to the throne but she wasn't good enough, in the eyes of the establishment, to become Queen of England.

The Queen, her sister, was the Head of The Church of England so Margaret marrying a divorced man was out of the question.

Princess Margaret would have suffered the same consequences as her uncle, the Duke of Windsor, before her. She would be stripped of her title Her Royal Highness and be forced to live in exile for the rest of her life if she married Townsend. In the end, she gave up the idea of ever marrying him.

She did finally marry Lord Snowdon but started an affair with Roddy Llewellyn in 1973. He was seventeen years younger than her. Her open relationship with him caused much embarrassment for the Royal Family and the newspapers were full of it. This affair finally ended the Margaret's marriage to Snowdon and she went on to live a very unhappy life.

She had been denied the right to marry her real love Peter Townsend.

There are many similarities, or if you like, coincidences which are going to appear throughout this book!

Diana was the third to follow suit.

Hypocrites

If we need to talk of hypocrisy we need to examine the British Royal Family and the Earl Spencer, Diana's brother.

The Queen of England is the Head of The Church of England and in the eyes of the church, divorced people could not re-marry in church. I have been married twice so I know what I am talking about. In my day you couldn't re-marry in the Church of England if you were divorced. Vows had been taken in the eyes of God that you were married "until death do you part."

It's strange, but after the Queen Mother's death in 2002, the Church of England changed its views on divorced people and now they are free to re-marry in church. So who changed the views? The Church of England or the Head of the Church of England?

How convenient now to change views, after all, it opened up the way for Charles, future king, to re-marry. Remember he was divorced from Diana before she died. All of the Queen's children are divorced except for Prince Edward. It's too much of a coincidence that views are changed and my opinion is that they were changed to suit the monarchy, for their convenience, but that's my opinion.

The Queen Mother was no longer alive so Charles could marry Camilla and not be afraid any more of upsetting his grandmother. Charles was her favourite grandson!

You have already read about how the Church of England felt about the events regarding the former King Edward VIII and Wallis Simpson. You have already read about the event regarding Princess Margaret and Peter Townsend. The Queen Mother is no longer with us so if views are changed in the eyes of the Church of England, the Charles and Camilla situation wouldn't be a problem. It would be convenient. Did the Church change its views to go along with modern times or what?

I call it hypocrisy!

Another hypocrite is Earl Spencer, Diana's brother. His emotional address during her funeral in Westminster Abbey when he said that "Diana didn't need a royal title," should have choked him!

When Diana was experiencing problems in her marriage she turned to her brother for help.

She wanted to return to live at Althorp House, the family's estate. He didn't want her there because he didn't want the paparazzi on his doorstep. He didn't want Althorp to become a tourist attraction. She was alive then.

How different after her death. Suddenly, he becomes interested in his sister. Now she's dead it's another story.

Diana is buried in the grounds of Althorp and because of her popularity in life many thousands of visitors go each year to visit her memorial site.

So now Althorp is a tourist attraction, something he didn't want when she was alive! It is now a big business, a money-maker.

DIANA, ANOTHER ROYAL SCANDAL

James Hewitt, a former lover of Diana indicated on British TV sometime after her funeral that he had received threats from the palace because of his affair with her. Apparently it is also claimed that he wanted to sell love letters from her. Is this hypocrisy?

There have been these situations which would have caused a lot of embarrassment for the Royal Family, and especially Diana's popularity which was having on the monarchy which we will now look at.

Peter Townsend didn't break up a marriage and neither did Wallis Simpson, but Princess Margaret suffered and so did the Duke of Windsor just because they loved divorced persons.

Wallis Simpson wasn't allowed the title Her Royal Highness because she was a divorced woman. If Princess Margaret had married Peter Townsend she would have lost her title Her Royal Highness. Diana lost her title Her Royal Highness after she divorced Charles yet Camilla has been given the title Her Royal Highness! What hypocrisy!!

On top of all that, the British taxpayers are maintaining her while she lives the life of Riley!

Is this justice?

The Queen should have made it clear to Charles that if he married Camilla he would have to face the music and give up his right to the throne and live in exile like his great uncle had to.

What's good enough for one should be good enough for another.

How could the Queen accept Camilla into the Royal Family after all the scandal knowing it could only have a damaging effect on them? Has she gone soft in her old age?

If Charles couldn't be loyal to Diana how, as King of England, can he be loyal to the Crown?

How can he be trusted to be Defender of the Faith when he was unfaithful to his fiancée on the eve of their wedding and all the time during their marriage? He should be given the title Defender of the Unfaithful!

How come Wallis Simpson wasn't given the title Her Royal Highness because she was divorced? How come Diana lost her title Her Royal Highness because she became divorced?

How come Camilla has been given the title Her Royal Highness when she is divorced? Sheer hypocrisy!!

William told his mother that he would give her back the title Her Royal Highness when he becomes king. Let's hope he does it posthumously.

After the Divorce

When a marriage has reached the point of break down and the point of no return it is devastating and deep wounds are inflicted on the person who is suffering the most – the innocent victim.

I know, I've been there and I'm certain that Diana must have been feeling the same. When the other person has betrayed you how can you feel?

When marriage vows are taken we vow to be with each other in sickness and in health, for better for worse until death us do part.

I'm sure that Diana tried to keep the marriage going even though she was aware of Charles' infidelity. Camilla was doing the same thing, cheating on her own husband too.

Diana wasn't the first to go through this painful experience and definitely won't be the last.

It's even worse when children are involved and also when someone like her is always in the public eye.

Everyone could see the pain she was suffering when she left the divorce courts. It was written all over her face. She was the innocent party and suffered for it. She came from a broken family and now felt like a failure because her own marriage had failed.

She had no support from the Royal Family and none from her own family so she must have felt very desperate. It was probably her children who kept her going. But nonetheless, she survived and knew that she had to get on with her life.

Maybe it was wrong of her to go public and accuse Charles on British TV of his adultery.

Maybe it was her way of getting revenge. At the end of the day it was a terrible experience for her.

After the divorce Charles still had custody of his children. I wasn't so lucky. When my first marriage ended, my ex-wife denied my access to my daughter. No matter how hard I tried the law, at that time was on the mother's side. Because I had no access to my own daughter, the grandparents on both sides suffered too. They didn't see their grandchild.

When I lost access to my daughter I was devastated. I had no motivation to live and I was completely destroyed emotionally and I was the innocent party! So yes, I can understand what Diana must have been going through and I'm sure that most of you readers who have experienced this can understand.

As the book began, time heals all pain and it took me a long time to overcome my time of despair. But life goes on. So Diana's life went on. She did a lot of good things for charity – she became Britain's ambassador, if you like, in work involved with charities.

Her compassion for people helped her survive. The British people loved and adored her even more. She became the Queen of Hearts even though she never became Queen of England.

A queen is usually given this title through heritage but Diana gained her title Queen of Hearts because of the love of the people and not just the people of England. She deserved this title and being Queen of Hearts was much more important to her than being Queen of England.

After the controversial interview with the BBC and after the divorce, Diana started to get on with her own life.

She was stripped of her title Her Royal Highness, but that didn't decrease her popularity level with the public. She was still Diana, royal title or not.

She continued her role in helping people who were less fortunate than herself and acted as an ambassador for England by getting more deeply involved with charity work.

The suffering of her marriage breakdown didn't change her natural personality. This work kept her going. She became the Queen of Hearts.

She also said that she lived for her sons and would be lost without them. She wanted them to be able to understand people's emotions and their insecurities, their distress, hopes and dreams.

However, she was now a free agent no longer shackled to the monarchy and had the freedom of speech, the freedom to do as she liked. She had developed into a mature woman so very different from the shy, young girl that she first was. The public could see this. She was very outspoken something that displeased the monarchy.

Britain is a democracy and has the freedom of speech but is talking about the monarchy in an open way democracy or treason?

If Diana had made the statements she made in the days of Queen Elizabeth I she would have gone straight to the Tower of London and eventually have been executed. The same goes for me. Had I written this book in those days I would have suffered the same fate.

So, Diana started a relationship with Dodi Fayed. There were many rumours going around at the time. and just previous to her death, that she and Dodi were going to get married and live in the former Duke of Windsor's home, the Villa Windsor, in France.

It has been claimed that she and Dodi had visited the Villa Windsor, planning to move there after they had been married. Could this have been an embarrassment for the monarchy?

It certainly would have opened up old wounds from the past.

If Diana had married Dodi she was still young enough to have children and he was also young. She would have probably changed her religion to that of a Muslim, which Dodi was.

Her children would have been half brothers or sisters to William and Harry.

Could this have been an embarrassment for the British monarchy?

After all is said and done she was still the mother of the future King of England, Head of the Church of England. The Head of the Church of England whose mother is now a Muslim!

Dead or alive, Diana is still the mother of the future King of England – we cannot deny this!

Close friends of Diana also believe and accept that Prince Harry was a love child and that his real father is James Hewitt, although James Hewitt has always denied this. She herself believed that he was Harry's father.

As Harry grew older he looked more and more like James Hewitt and people say that there is a remarkable resemblance.

A quote from the National Examiner said: "As Diana's power over the public grew stronger, powerful forces behind the British throne saw her more and more as a threat."

A letter written in Diana's own handwriting was published claiming that Charles was planning to kill her in a car accident but this was not made public until after her death.

Another report stated that Diana was afraid of Prince Philip. The Queen's husband, and was reported that she told one of her closest friends just before she died that she thought Philip would do something bad against her if she didn't sleep with him.

This is very difficult to believe but who knows?

If this was true and Diana made this public, further embarrassment would have fallen on the monarchy.

Diana was becoming more and more outspoken and needed to be shut up!

Rumours also had it that on her return from Paris that fateful weekend, she was going to tell the nation something that was going to shock them but she never lived to tell the tale.

Diana's Death

I personally never met Diana or saw her in person but for me she was like a member of my own family. I am sure that many people feel the same way. This is the effect she had on people, the charisma that radiated from her. She was the epitome of a princess.

Her tragic death in 1997 left me feeling grief stricken. I felt as if I had lost someone very close. This effect was felt by the entire nation. The nation was in a state of shock.

The country had never seen such an open display of grief as on the scale of Diana's death.

To die so tragically and so young and full of life was devastating. I remember very well how I heard about her death. My neighbour came knocking my door on the Sunday morning with the news. I couldn't believe it until I turned on the TV and saw it for myself. All the channels were full of the news. In the town where I lived, all the public buildings had the Union Flag flying at half mast, constantly reminding us of the tragedy. The town square was filled with bouquets of flowers with notes to Diana, just like we were seeing outside of Buckingham Palace.

I remember signing the Book of Condolence in the town hall. I doubt very much that the British people will ever see such a public showing of emotion again.

Diana made history and I was there to see history in the making.

Diana believed in astrologers and clairvoyants and was known to have consulted them on various occasions. It seems very strange too that her car crashed into the 13th pillar in the tunnel in Paris. 13 being an unlucky and superstitious number.

It has also been revealed that a police official in Wales had a premonition of her death, so why didn't he make it public at the time? Why wait until after the event?

It's okay to make these announcements after something has happened just to get publicity!

At the time of her death the popularity of the monarchy dwindled and people were crying out for a referendum to see if the monarchy was still worth having. Tony Blair didn't think that this was a good idea being well aware of public feeling at the time.

Maybe if there had been a referendum the monarchy would have ceased to exist. Again, who knows?

In my opinion, along with many others, I think that the Royal Family is a waste of money but of course there are others who don't agree. Tony Blair's wife, Cheryl, was of the same mind.

She had no time for them and this was made quite evident in the movie The Queen, which we will go on to talk about.

The Movie

The movie, made by Pathe and Granada, was a very good movie indeed but what was it representing? It started off with the newly elected Prime Minister Tony Blair and from then on focused on Diana's death.

It is a movie showing us the Royal Family's reaction to her death. Well, there are two sides to a coin and the film only showed us one side – the Royal Family's.

While the Queen obviously gave her permission are we really seeing what went on behind the scenes or are we seeing what the Royal Family want us to see?

We can plainly see the attitude of Prince Philip but it has always been common knowledge that he can be a very arrogant man.

Nobody is perfect but it was clear to me that he didn't like Diana at all.

Prince Charles looked very edgy knowing that the public was against him and was sucking up to Tony Blair for support. This is all his deep set feeling of guilt on how he had treated Diana.

It was obvious that the royals didn't care about what had happened to her. They showed no sense of remorse.

Eventually, the Queen was pressurized to return to London to face the British public and she was very worried about the feeling of the public toward the monarchy.

I was living in England at that time and I remember the people calling to abolish the monarchy. At the time, one in four of the population were in favour of abolishing it and seventy per cent said that the Queen's attitude had damaged the monarchy.

She had every right to be concerned.

When she made her tribute to Diana, Downing Street added "and as a grandmother," to it to make it sound more meaningful. The tribute was something that the Queen had to make because of the public outcry. The same went for the flying of the Union Jack at half-mast above Buckingham Palace. The monarchy has never been so close to becoming non-existent as at that time.

So, we only saw the Royal Family's side. Why didn't we see the Spencer's side of the story?

Why didn't we see the Fayed's side of the story? I'm sure that the Fayed's would have liked to have been involved in the movie. After all, Dodi's father has spent a lot of money trying to get to the bottom of this accident. Is somebody trying to hide something?

So in the end, was the movie trying to show us that Tony Blair had gained more respect from the public than the Queen and this had been gained at the expense of Diana's death?

The movie should have showed all sides of the story, even Camilla's side of it. It's something worth considering.

Cause for
Embarrassment?

Diana was an embarrassment for the Royal Family because she developed from a shy, young girl into a very outspoken woman. The public could see this. Diana had something in common with Charles' aunt, Princess Margaret, who also caused embarrassment for the

Royal Family with her much publicized romantic affairs, especially the one with Roddy Llewellyn.

Now Diana, had she married Dodi Fayed, would this be yet another embarrassment for the House of Windsor? After all, she is the mother of the future King of England.

Is the marriage of Charles and Camilla an embarrassment? Of course not. It turned out to be very convenient. Why didn't he marry her before? Had he married Camilla before, whether or not it upset his grandmother, The Queen Mother, none of this tragedy would have happened.

Diana wouldn't have become a princess and William wouldn't have been born, therefore no heir to the throne.

Any embarrassment to the Royal Family has been brought on to them by themselves – history has been made!!

Had Diana married Dodi Fayed, she would have probably changed her religion and become Muslim. Still young enough to have children, they would have been half-brothers or half-sisters to Princes William and Harry, both of royal blood.

William will one day become King of England, if the British monarchy survives, and will automatically become the Head of the Church of England. Could this have been a cause of embarrassment as the King of England's mother is a Muslim?

Who Is to Blame?

B ut will we ever know what really happened? It was a verdict
of accidental death.

There are still many questions that have gone unanswered.

Why did they let someone they knew was drunken drive the
car? Anyone in their right mind would never get into a car with
a drunk driver and risk their lives. If her bodyguard was aware of
this then why did he allow it?

Diana was a very important person to have had her life put
at such a risk.

Why did it take so long for her to be taken to hospital for
emergency treatment? If I had been involved in a road traffic
accident I would have been taken to the nearest emergency room
for treatment.

The doctor who treated Diana at the scene of the accident
said that she had a chance of survival.

An ambulance arrived at the scene fifteen minutes after the
crash but the paramedics spent almost one hour treating her,
which was far too long. She should have been taken immediately
to the nearest hospital for emergency treatment to stop the
internal bleeding she had suffered as a result.

The hospital, Piete-Saltpetriere was 6.5 kilometres away
from the scene of the accident and a normal journey in an

emergency would have taken between five and ten minutes. The ambulance drove slowly and it wasn't until forty minutes later that it arrived. The question is: why did it take so long for it to get there especially with a very important person seriously injured on board?

Diana suffered major thoracic trauma and a dislocated shoulder along with an internal lesion.

The internal bleeding led to a cardiac arrest which claimed her life. So the cause of death was internal bleeding.

The cause of the deaths of the chauffeur Henri Paul and Dodi Fayed were similar. They both had ruptures in the isthmus of the aorta and fractured spines.

But Diana could have been saved and lived to have told the tale.

Were Diana and Dodi in the wrong place at the wrong time or were they in the right place at the right time?

Why didn't Diana and Dodi stay at the hotel that night?

Paris is a lively city, full of night life so where was everybody on the night of the accident?

It seems very strange that the car carrying Diana was apparently the only one in the tunnel at the time of the accident.

If people knew that Henri Paul, the chauffeur, was way over the limit to drive her car he should have been stopped. By allowing him to drive the car Diana's death warrant had been signed.

If he was to blame for the accident the verdict should have been manslaughter – the crime of killing a person illegally but not intentionally.

It was claimed that he was well over the legal limit so why didn't the verdict state manslaughter?

Perhaps if an open verdict had been reached, this would have resulted in the belief that there had been a conspiracy.

It results in many people still believing that Diana's death is like a jigsaw puzzle. Some pieces have gone missing so the jigsaw will never be completed.

The dictionary definition of accident is: an unpleasant event happening unexpectedly or by chance.

Henri Paul, as it has been claimed, was drunk so the likelihood of having an accident was very high, so if it was an accident did he cause it? My reply would be yes, because he lost control of the car so he caused the accident by driving while under the influence of alcohol and driving without due care and attention.

If he didn't cause it who or what did?

It is a well-known fact that the French have a strong dislike for the English. This goes back centuries so there would have been no love lost in public relations between the two countries over this tragedy.

Diana was an English princess – dubbed England's Rose in the song by Elton John – the same song he wrote about Marilyn Monroe but with different words.

The paparazzi were immediately blamed for causing the accident by chasing after her for photos. Newspapers are made to sell stories that is why they are printed.

Then, the chauffeur was blamed because he was driving while drunk.

It is very easy to blame someone else for something that has happened but who really was to blame?

The British verdict was manslaughter. So she was killed but not intentionally!

Diana thought that she had nothing to lose by making her views about the monarchy public, but she lost her life and was silenced forever. No more embarrassment for the Royal Family and anyway what do they care about public opinion?

It appears that the only people satisfied with the verdict were the Royal Family. Henri Paul's family apparently weren't satisfied with the French side of things. Dodi Fayed's father definitely wasn't satisfied with the outcome and who knows what the Spencer family thought.

Why was Charles allowed to go to identify Diana's body and escort it back to England? He was no longer legally married to her. Was it a sense of guilt or did he just want to make sure she was now out of the way?

Fine, she was given a State Funeral but why wasn't she allowed to lie in State? The people would have been able to have paid their last respects to a woman they adored so much.

Diana and Marilyn Monroe had things in common.

They were both famous blondes. They were both 36 when they died. They both died in tragic and mysterious circumstances. They were both involved with prominent public figures and they both had the same song dedicated to them by Elton John – Candle in the Wind.

Marilyn Monroe was a queen in her own rights – a Hollywood movie queen.

Diana was the Queen of Hearts.

Almost 25 years on

Prince William, her son, is now married to Kate Middleton, the future King and Queen of England. They do have things in common and they have something in their favour – they are the same age – not the 12 years difference as was William's father in relation to his mother.

William resembles Diana a lot. If he has a similar personality and remains close and in touch with his people, as was his mother, he will be a very popular and well-loved king.

If the House of Windsor is to survive, the responsibility will be his and Kate's.

We have to remember that at the end of the day public opinion can change and we are now in the 21st century and there may well come the day when the British no longer want a monarchy.

This almost happened back in 1997 when public feeling about the monarchy ran high and people were calling for a referendum. This gave cause for concern for the Queen.

What would happen to them? Where would they live? Nothing is guaranteed in times of change.

Charles and Camilla should be stripped of their titles HRH and be banished from the country and made to live in exile as was his great uncle Edward VIII and Wallis Simpson in the 1930s. They were guilty of adultery and should pay for it.

Charles should never be allowed to become King of England and the throne should pass on to William.

Parliament has the power to do this. The Royal Family are a status symbol and nothing more.

What will happen to Camilla when and if Charles becomes king? Will she be known as the Consort Stepmother? What a way to go down in history!

The British monarchy has become a laughing stock in the eyes of the world.

The Head of State, whether it is a king or a queen, is just a Head of State. People vote for a government and in Britain's case the head of the government, the Prime Minister is the leader of the country and has the power to do as he or she wishes.

People do not vote for a king or a queen and the voice of the people can force a government to take action and make changes and one of these changes could be to abolish the monarchy once and for all.

This is the people's decision!

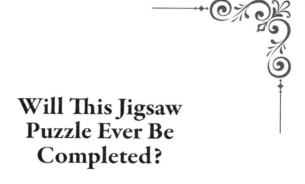

Will This Jigsaw Puzzle Ever Be Completed?

When you are constructing a jigsaw puzzle, you need all of the pieces to complete it. When some pieces go missing the puzzle cannot be completed so we have to guess or imagine what the final picture is going to look like with the information that we have. Apparently, French death certificates do not show a cause of death and apart from close family requests all information remains confident for one hundred years.

It's like the Sleeping Beauty fairy-tale. The only problem here is that Diana won't wake up after one hundred years has passed, but perhaps the truth will come to light in 2097 about the mystery surrounding her death.

Then, and only then, her great grandchildren and the public will be awakened to this mystery.

Maybe then the missing piece of this jigsaw puzzle will be put into place and the picture will finally become clear and the truth will be uncovered.

But will there still be a monarchy in Britain in the year 2097?

Reflections

In 2022, Queen Elizabeth II will celebrate seventy years on the throne. She is the longest living monarch to have served longer than Queen Victoria.

Let's hope that in the run up to the celebrations of this and to mark the 25th anniversary of the death of Diana, she can reflect on her seventy years as monarch and the things that have caused scandal within the Royal Family during her reign and maybe she will get closer to her people, as did Diana.

The monarchy needs to modernize if it is to survive.

Conclusion

I have always believed that there is always some truth behind a rumour and that the truth always hurts.

Now that you have finished reading this book you can draw your own conclusions. The book is only my opinion but my final question is: "Will we ever discover the truth about Diana's death?"

Don't miss out!

Visit the website below and you can sign up to receive emails whenever David J Cooper publishes a new book. There's no charge and no obligation.

https://books2read.com/r/B-A-CBBF-KEVMB

BOOKS 2 READ

Connecting independent readers to independent writers.

Also by David J Cooper

Penny Lane, Paranormal Investigator
The Witch Board
The House of Dolls
The House of Dolls
The Devil's Coins
The Mirror
The Key
The Reveal

Standalone
The Devil Knows
The Party's Over
Encuentro Mortal
Se Acabo La Fiesta
Cold Fury
Deadly Encounter
House on the Hill
Diana, another Royal scandal

Watch for more at davidjcooperauthorblog.wordpress.com.

About the Author

David J Cooper is a British author. He was born in Darlaston, West Midlands, to a working class family. After leaving school he had jobs ranging from engineering to teaching. He got involved in local politics and became a local councillor in 1980.

His novels incorporate elements of the paranormal, horror, suspense, and mystery.

He is featured in the Best Poems and Poets of 2012 with his first and only poem God's Garden.

He currently lives in a small town in Mexico with his three dogs, Chula, Sooty, and Benji.

Read more at davidjcooperauthorblog.wordpress.com.

Printed in Great Britain
by Amazon